THE HIDDEN WORLD

LEILA PEPPER

Leila Pepper

National Library of Canada Cataloguing in Publication

Pepper, Leila
        The hidden world / Leila Pepper.

Poems.
ISBN 0-88753-373-6

        I. Title.

PS8581.E633H44 2002   C811'.54   C2002-903038-2
PR9199.3.P424H44 2002

The Palm Poets Series is published by Black Moss Press at
2450 Byng Road, Windsor, Ontario N8W 3E8. Black Moss
books are distributed in Canada and the U.S. by Firefly Books,
3680 Victoria Park Ave., Willowdale, Ont. Canada. All orders
should be directed there.

Black Moss would like to acknowledge the generous support
of the Canada Council and the Ontario Arts Council for its
publishing program.

Le Conseil des Arts | The Canada Council
        du Canada | for the Arts

ONTARIO ARTS COUNCIL
CONSEIL DES ARTS DE L'ONTARIO

(I)

Survival

The Breakfast Room

Pierre Bonnard: 1867-1947

"His fascination was with light
and its play on everyday things.
For him a painting was a
stilling of time
a sensation caught forever."

I am immersed in the warmth
of his everyday life
here a table
on its striped cloth
fruit and fish
biscuits and small rolls
there a hint of latticed wallpaper
and a glimpse of his greening garden
all friendly and familiar
all suffused with light
suggesting an intimacy I share
for as I watch I am there
quiet and unobserved

this stilling of time is
what we try for as we write
our thoughts and feelings
caught forever

6

The Hidden World

Paul advising the Colossians:
By Him all things were created
that are in Heaven and Earth
... visible and invisible

I am aware a secret world exists
this glittering night city is
superimposed upon a hidden place
where timber wolves, brush wolves
and coyotes used to hunt
mating and foraging in packs
We usurped their land   piece
by piece   stole it from them
pushing them back as we settled in

When I read Paul's words
"visible and invisible" I tremble
such hidden life overwhelms me
fills me with fear and wonder
all around us this other world
moves in its darkness

we only see animals in city zoos
or copies made for children
to cuddle in warm beds   but
the hidden ones are not toys
wherever they have gone
they are animals that must kill
to survive   their need goes on
by day and night   they move
eyes glittering   stealthy
in their secret ways   avoiding
our unwelcome presence
shadows upon my visible world
shadows I cannot see but sense
knowing I share their instincts
their compulsions

8

Strange New World

With the Orbital Space Telescope
scientists have peered
thirteen billion years
back in time to find
a galaxy "fizzing" with stars
new ones near the edge
of the universe
but I thought
Eternity was limitless!
was this how people felt when
they learned our world was round
perplexed and filled with doubts
everything turned upside down?
still   the thought of
fizzing stars makes me feel safe
some giant hand must have
shaken them up   tossed them
into the distant sky
for me to stare at
in endless wonderment

Thread of Continuity

Dead as a dodo
we've all said it
the name is synonymous
with extinction
or was until today
scientists believe that
by extracting DNA from
the preserved head and foot
of the last-ever dodo
they can resurrect
this vanished bird
Matching its unique genes
with those of
closely-allied species
they hope
to close the gap left
in the world's ecosystem
by the dodo's demise

10

if this bird   why not me?
a resurrection
with infinite variations
from descendents who
would then be ancestors
but   would it really be me?
after centuries in the ground
what could resurrection mean?
would this creature look like me
move as I move   think as I think
could I say where I have been
in all those lost years
in the dark earth
would my words be understood
who would know me?

Three A.M.

restless I wake
the night thick around me
lights from a car
break the darkness
then pass slowly by

I remember summers ago
in the cottage by the lake
when a wild storm cut all
power to the town and we
watched black night invade
no gleam of light
from far-off windows
no sound of waves
when the storm passed -
unnatural silence held us
captives of time
we filled the big room
with candles   every stub
we could find so

outlined faces glowed
as we moved about
dancing shadows large
across the wooden walls
oh we were safe inside
safe against the crushing dark!

alone and restless
I look out now
into an empty night

13

Ubi Sunt: The Wanderer c. 900 A.D.

I found it this morning
a scrap of paper
notes from my
Early English Studies
reading it   I have a longing
to start again   to share
that changeless lament

        hwaer cwom mearg
        what has become of the horse
        of the kinsman
        of the glorious lord?
        how that time has disappeared
        grown dark with cover of night
        as though it never was

and I sit here
close to tears
what can I add
to this universal cry
where has it all gone?

The Astronaut's Love Song

To venture into space
like Daedalus on unsure wings
facing possible death
is an acceptable concept
there is blood-stirring challenge
there and certain glory
I could approach the take-off calmly
knowing that above the shouting
and acclaim   the cameras and mikes
she would be waiting my return
but never for me frozen flight
suspended in uncertainty
five-hundred cryogenic years
wakening to
Rip van Winkle resurrection
in an alien world
the thought is monstrous
I could accept my love's tears
salt on my lips as we said
goodbye before take-off

but to be in a universe where
not even old men would mumble her name
in questioning and rheumy syllables
waken to a place   in which
she did not exist
this is the desolation
I could not face

16

Trompe-l'Oeil

From my window
to the east I see
a world on fire
it's not the ordered sun
breaking its rule but
autumn maple leaves
glowing like flames
against the darkening sky
as I watch
they become smudges
on the horizon
now I remember
John Donne's defiant challenge
"busy old fool, unruly sun"
and find wry comfort
in his impudent words
Dr. Donne   great preacher
my plain John Donne   a poet
torn between flesh and spirit
loving the carnal world

yet loving God   pouring out
his eternal battle   in
the burning Holy Sonnets
begging leave to love
in wonder asking his God
"wilt Thou forgive?"
as I do for my own strong doubts
chorusing with him the fear
I too shall perish
on the farthest shore
he speaks for me who
celebrated all his joys
and for the self-same sins
must ask forgiveness
in the dying sun

18

Memory and Daffodils

faint odour of daffodils
picked after rain
and on the T.V. screen
demonstrating "intelligence"
a neurologist
slices through the sample
displayed on a metal table
saying
this is the brain
of an elderly person
while he meticulously cuts
a pink pulpy sponge
using an electric saw
carves it into quarters
as if he holds
a piece of meat
on a butcher's slab
points out
the Valley of Memory

whose old thoughts
whose old desires
whose forgotten love
lie there?
if it were mine
would I   body gone
be conscious
feel pain in my head
as I am exhibited
to a Freshman class?

20   tell them I remember
rain-washed daffodils
please say
she has gone away
she is not here

Does Death Come Easily?

for F.B.

On the phone this morning
she told me he was dead
I heard her weeping
felt her tears as if
they were warm on my hands
I'm sorry   so sorry
inadequate words
to assuage grief

Now as I scrub the floor
and polish the sink
I wonder if
death comes easily
like rolling over or
turning out the light?
wonder further if
this frantic work I do
staves off my own mortality

makes death   his or mine
unreal   a story
someone will tell
in another place
at another time?

22

A Dead Rat

the rat
lay on the road
two drops of blood
oozing from its nostrils
how transitory life is
one moment my old cat
warm in my arms
the next
light gone from
his golden eyes
instant stillness
instant ceasing
a blown candle
only memories
drifting like smoke

Fate

Eagerly
the ant climbed my breadboard
to cross new-found territory
just before I flattened him
with a well-aimed blow
which was all it took
to reduce this explorer
to a speck of black
how random!   how final!
I wonder
will it be the same for me?
In an unexpected moment
one blow from above
as sudden   as careless
as the quietus of the ant
will be my own death

The Eternal Question

Stretched across the bed
with my little dog I lie
and watch the autumn clouds
drift down a windless sky

countless people pass
an ever-flowing stream
tangible as earth and iron
yet formless as a dream

a host will follow after
as a host has gone ahead
pondering on Eternity
when dog and I are dead

Immediacy

(to Ernest Dowson)

Fear will not let me say it
but thoughts run free
yes they are not long
these days   for wine and roses
or for me
speak to me
touch me
while we can
the long days come later
that form Eternity

Descending the Stairs

Something
about the way the sun
shines on the wall
highlighting each step
stops me
makes me stand still
and think
how we take it for granted
that all will endure
my house   my books
my pictures hanging there
forever and ever
but that stab of light
hits hard
pushes mortality in my face
reminds me
I am a transient
on a temporary pass

Entrapment

The air in the room heavy
with the odour of flowers
stifles her
at her shoulder
she hears the menace
of an old man's whisper
'Your generation
you're the next wave'
an unknown sea swells over her
carried along   struggling
in the swift momentum
choking   blinded by salt spray
she is held at the crest
for a breathless moment
sees people beside her
all around her
before she is
propelled relentlessly forward
towards a dark horizon
a dark and distant shore

there is nothing else here but
the sickening smell of flowers
and her own despair   she is
trapped by the coffin
there is no escape   no corner free

The Anniversary

last night
our music

so I danced alone
turning   turning
with quick sure steps
last night alone
I felt your presence
ghostly those arms
illusory
last night alone
dancing
we danced

Where Do The Days Go?

Last week was Thanksgiving
today I sit on the bank
the grass around me
butter-yellow with leaves
shaken from the basswood tree
and it seems a year ago
ten years ago
all the years of my life
where do the days go?

driftwood on the beach
water retreating stones stand
high and moss-exposed
on ribbed brown sand
in the ragged wind-torn garden
pod and root alike lie bare
the wind has a faint breath of cold
that the warm sun tries to exorcise
ghostly warning of winter to come

they came in laughing
young arms spilling over
with gourds and melons
with grapes and firm apples
awkward stalks of corn
and golden pumpkin to
mountain a centrepiece on
the polished oak table
made by my father's hands
sixty years ago of his eighty
what remain but the table and
a headstone in a grove of trees?

restless candle-flames stir
shadows on beloved faces and
this is the real Thanksgiving
some of them will inherit my days
will remember my voice
let it be my children's children
cradled only in the heart now
who will say grace here for
a time they cannot remember
Eternity is a pattern
this is where the days go

Houses

this one
a sturdy place
where lead-glass windows
cast prisms on the rug
small rainbows
dancing in the sun

my great-grandmother's fire screen
with stitches so delicate
they could be painted there—
still stands protecting after
a hundred and fifty years
the log-cabin she came to first
was small and cold   she wept
for Ireland and her old home
and I can feel her sadness when
I hold her ivory fan   her mute guitar
her tiny crystal perfume bottles
made to dangle from one's finger
on a golden ring

on my wall hangs the portrait
of the gentleman in faded ruff
whose stern eyes followed me
across our dining-room
when I was young
back and forth   back and forth
we went   and I could swear
eyes and lips moved
but not in smiling

there in the hall you see
the walnut washstand we bought
for our first house, to hold
new china and shinging silver,
unpolished and unused today

now up the stairs past
the fading Egyptian water-colour
the political cartoons from France
all three my mother's heritage
and into the guestroom to view
the fourposter bed where I was born
too soon and had no cradle
only my father's leather chair

34

here is my own room where
I lie alone under the quilt
passed for five generations
from mother to daughter
so not really mine
these tangibles weave an intangible past
though each room is loud with memories
the house itself is silent
it knows what changes lie ahead

35

Solving the Riddle of the Ages

National Geographic, September 2001

a summary:
how old is anything?
the oldest rock?
perhaps more than
four billion years
humans?

there is a special pattern in
the decomposition of the body
the common blow-fly uncannily
attracted to carrion and blood
is almost always first
at the scene of a death
so there I lie
bare bones on a table
a skeleton
stripped within days
yet   so I am told

all the atoms of my body
have been wandering through the air
and the ground and the deep ocean
for billions of years
and even before then
they were made in stars
out of other atoms
which reach far back to
the first second of the universe
when all matter came into being

Science tells me <u>what</u> I am
but who can tell me <u>who</u> I am?

In Old Age

Today the first cold
of Autumn hit us
I thought I saw brown leaves
blown through my garden-gate
but these were birds low-flying
small finches   a flock of them
caught on their way South
as surprised as we by cold
I crumbled oat-bread
to toss outside
thirty or forty birds
flew down like arrows
from the bushes
to feast on stale crumbs
a black squirrel joined them
I who have been to London
to Paris and to Rome
felt such happiness here
I wanted to shout
See! I am alive
I am still with you

The Old Garden

Desolate the garden
on this cold March day
all my birds are gone
the empty feeder sways
in a small wind that
skirls dry leaves
as it passes
everything is grey
even the sky is leaden
but Spring will come again
already
willow branches are yellow
crocus and scilla
daffodil and hyacinth
are waiting in the wings
so much promise here
that I am bold to hope
once more
I'll dance with them

(II)

Vignettes

Betrayed

Your eyes clear water
no warning winter's coming
would turn them to ice

Loss

O my diminished world!
I thought I saw his profile
in the morning crowd.

44

G.K.D.

Nothing has changed
From your window
long shadows spread
across the midnight lawn
the moon spills silver
on the dark lake
As I stand here
the scent of roses
drifts up
from the old garden
nothing has changed
I said
but you are not here
and never will be again

Hot Summer Nights

nightmare heat
the mind lethargic
as the heavy body
somewhere far off
a piano sounds
cool jazz
music I remember
from years ago
remember
moving to the rhythm
our young bodies
unaware of summer
feeling another heat

Late August Beach

I have a feeling
this is where memory
will return to linger
in later years   return
to this beach
the mist   the chilly air
this circle on the sand
somewhere in the dark
a paddle dips and lifts
a faint ripple laps
the midnight shore and
voices rise in song
the dying fire
casts strange shadows
on faces leaning close
never again this night
never again his hands
touching her soft young hair

"Spanish Is A Loving Tongue"

In seventeenth century Madrid
Calderon de la Barca wrote
"La Vida Es Sueño"
a poetic play on the
ultimate meaning of life
I studied it
a long time ago   but
it didn't reach me until tonight
carefully washing supper dishes
rinsing off the soap
I feel unreal   temporary
I am here in the kitchen
yet I am there too
in the class room
young and in love and
Spanish is the language of love
"mi amor   mi corazón"
I have forgotten his face
but the memory is here
the feeling of it is here

the pain and the beauty
how short the time!
how right the poet
who asks "Que es la vida?"
and answers himself
"Toda la vida es sueño"
"life is a shadow   a dream"
and passes like a dream

"In This Transitory Life"

Early morning dark
in India
two crowded trains collide
cars flip over
crumple like paper
burst into flames
and hundreds die
Safe in my bed
a continent away
I hear the news
and I am full
of questions:
who was watching over them
who ignored
their cries for help
their screams?
was He asleep or deaf
or just too far away?
It seems there
are no answers

no comfort in
this random world
where through shame
I dare not ask for rain
relief from heat
or
from my body's pain

51

"We Are Sharply In Life"

the funeral cortege snails its way
along the sun-drenched street
no leaf turns   no bird sings
a sudden stillness of nature
mourns this stranger
pays him momentary homage
then the ice-cream wagon's bell
rings on the air   fills it with
the surge of childrens' feet and
the sound of their high-pitched voices
all around life starts again

Holy Icons

Madonna and Child
painted in oils
carved in wood
shaped in marble
they are everywhere
and soon in
this coming cold season
will be multiplied
on greeting cards

in church today
I saw another side
a small boy held close
in his father's arms
so much trust   so much love
that the pure warmth when
they looked at each other
drew me in

Rorie: 1985-2000

We were so comfortable
my cat and I
old troupers
we shared routines
we shared my bed
and when it stormed
we shared our fear
he was stubborn too
knew what he wanted
knew what he didn't like
the whistling kettle
was worst of all
when I left it on
he'd climb the stairs
to tell me so
but he was always here
always at the door
when I came home
somehow though small

he filled the house
Since yesterday
it has grown too big
an enormous place
quiet and empty
like my heart

For Rorie: 1985-2000

a book of snapshots
on the table there
cold comfort
after fifteen years
I can retrace in it
our days together
from a tumbling kitten
to a grave old cat
but I can't feel him
know the comfort
of the steady purr   hear
footsteps on the stairs
or in the night
turn to the warmth
the softness of him
beside me on the bed

I Sit Here Drinking My Coffee

I am thinking:
these rugs
are definitely shabby
the ottoman needs repairs
and new covers would
improve my aging couch
sun struggles through
opaque windows   casting
dusty shadows on the floor
and outside
autumn grass grows tall
then I read the news:
in cyclone-ravaged Eastern India
bloated bodies   human corpses
lie rotting beside
the carcasses of
drowned cows and goats
so many thousands dead
there is no-one to cremate them
the stench of rotting flesh
portends epidemic
and in my cup
the coffee grows cold

View From A Window

You stride down the street
wind in your hair
shoulders squared to the world
I don't know who you are but
you know where you are going
and from the eagerness in your walk
there must be a woman waiting
.... I remember other days
and how quickly a young man
climbed the long stairway
to our first apartment
I should feel gnawing envy
but memory fills my heart
so sweetly that watching you
I am in love again

Poet Manqué

She produced
beautiful images
phrases to envy
we were enchanted
by what she said
but always and forever
the body of each poem
stayed in her head

Divorcee

She is so earnest   so beautiful
holding my hand   she says
"this will help arthritis
you take plump raisins
golden ones   put them
in a glass container
no other will do
pour in gin
enough to cover
soak them for seven days
stirring faithfully
after the seventh day
and not before
eat them seven at a time
until they are all gone
it helps   I swear
it helps the pain"

although to size and number
I've no chart
no eye of newt nor toe of frog
nor lizard's heart
I will mix her witches' brew
for if by taking it
I ease the pain or
heal the wounds
of her divorce
my twisted fingers
will stir faithfully
I will be dizzy with devotion
drunk for her cure

Having To Put My Dog To Sleep

I always thought
that you and I
in some far distant time
would die together
I pictured us
carved on a Medieval tomb
I with hands neatly folded
you curled at my feet
never to be separated
My small shadow
who mourned when I left
and leaped in ecstasy
each time we met again
five minutes or a day apart
worshipping with
eager tongue and eyes
the only deity you knew.

I wish I could believe
you stand
in some sky-wide window
your tail a quivering plume
of expectation as
you wait the footsteps
that you love . . .
little dog
your god begs
to be forgiven

November 11, 2000

the flag-draped coffin
inches past
why are they doing it
clapping for a corpse
clapping for a boy
who died fighting
for King and Country
sixty years ago?
I knew some of those boys
grew up with them
danced with them
waved goodbye at the station
wrote to them   wept for them
mourned them   but
we were young then
my Unknown Soldier
lies in dignity
in Westminster Abbey
under the flag he fought for
a different one

is this clapping
a heart-felt tribute
to bravery and commitment
or is there a sense
of manoeuvring here
some political aspect
that holds me today
frozen and unfeeling?

65

Black Dog

The friend who used to say
this too shall pass away
has been dead for twenty years

when he came ashore
during the war
there were always
celebrations
drinks and long talks
in wardrooms   in hotels
wherever we could meet
As the night wore on
"Down, Boy!" he would shout
"Down, Boy!"

I still hear the black dog
of his drunken imagination
barking at my heart

Cancer

For G.K.D.

Do I carry in me
the seeds of your destruction?
when I feel most sturdy
I remember
how much you loved life
and how well you used it
remember the quiet way
you left us that last hour
your pulse a small bird
fluttering   passing softly
almost imperceptibly
your joy and music gone
if I inherit those deadly seeds
let me carry also
the seeds of your courage
and your constant love

Concert: February, 2002

When I lie dying
let there be music
something
the heart remembers
perhaps I shall smell lavender
and think
half-dreaming
as darkness comes
Yes!
this is the right way home

68

Wintering

Fall had long come
waves claimed the cold shore
the day we closed the cottage
packed everything away
put up the storms
locked the door
turning the final key
Not until Spring
would we find out
that small bright eyes
had watched our backs
go down the cobblestone path
whiskers had twitched
Just ahead lay
thick mattresses
soft pillows   empty drawers
crumbs in dark corners
rustly paper for nests
and everywhere
silence
long lovely silence
as the sojourners settled in
prepared for their routine
of wintering in the cottage.

(III)

A Little Elocution

I Should Have Written It Down

I should have written it down
I know I should have
I'll regret it all my life
we were saying goodbye at the station
he said it as he turned away
there were crowds around us
and I wanted to hear his words
but my heart was pounding
my eyes were flooding and
the noise was an ocean's roar
so I shouted as I waved goodbye
"Darling, I'll never forget that
I'll keep it forever . . ."
and I know I will
warmed like a nestling
housed in my heart . . .
but he was disappearing
lost in the moving crowd
head and shoulders growing smaller

Does he really think of me that way?
am I? . . .how did he put it?
I was so thrilled I thought
I'll never <u>never</u> forget that
Am I really breathlessly *something*?
or *something ... something* exciting?
what was it about my eyes?
how did he put it?
the train was whistling
the conductor shouting
people shoving us apart
I should have written it down
I really should have!

74

Donna Roma, You Are Enthroned In My Heart

Donna Roma was beautiful
she wore silk stockings and
high-heels in Grade 6
while the rest of us
were in ankle-socks and loafers
she had a tiny waist and a wide
studded belt to cinch it in
we were thick in the middle
round with puppy-fat
at least I was and had freckles
and a short Dutch bob
Donna Roma had curls that bounced
and she flirted with all the boys
. . . and none of us liked her
then one day in class the teacher said
she had something sad to tell us
and it was that Donna Roma had died
we were all shocked . . .
<u>no one</u> died that young

but I didn't shed a tear for Donna Roma
I don't remember if any of us did
when I think of her today and of
how young she was all those years ago
I have a strange feeling of guilt
the sense of something left unsaid

Sermons

As the voice from the pulpit
drones on   I watch
the boy in the pew ahead
the boy with the horn
the shiny new Christmas one
oblivious to his parents' nudges
he is testing it silently
feeling it on his lips
making weird faces
bounding with terrible energy
Over and above me
I hear the words
"In the Beginning"
and I am the boy
leaping now
from pew to pew
racing the aisles
blowing my golden trumpet
to waken the dead
and the astonished parishioners
turn open-mouthed
as I rush past
out the church doors
and far away

Guilt

It is noon
I've walked twelve blocks
in the heat
and I'm tired
but across the street
the new Greek restaurant
is challenging me
it displays
a hopeful sign
    OPEN
it is very empty
behind those glistening windows
not a trace of movement
I know the menu
I could eat spinach pie
salad with feta and black olives
perhaps allow a taste
a mere crumb
of sinful baklava

but   I'm not really hungry
just very tired and the
grocery bags gain weight
with every step I take
I could eat the pie later
heat it for supper but
that means crossing the road
this is really depressing
one willing person   one pie
won't buy the owners a future
and that is the sad part
knowing
nothing I do matters
I can't save them

The Dieter's Kingdom
Of Earthly Delight

In my next incarnation   I shall be
the Fat Lady in the Circus
No need to diet   my fans will come
to admire my billows and curves
Fluffy and flirtatious   drowned in
pink ruffles I shall bask in
their admiration   when I clap my hands
trays will appear steaming and redolent
loaded with chicken wings and spare ribs
with pork chops and roast turkey
I shall wave away in moments
mere appetizers   cheese and oyster pate
smoked salmon and big black olives
to reach for slabs of fresh hot bread
dripping with golden butter
reach for steaming gravy
to smother the bread
O! the odours! the delicious odours!
I am dizzy with desire   what need

for cocktails in this intoxicating place?
I will attack the entrees with both hands
Away with pasta   with penne and rigatoni
mere ticklers of the appetite
Bring on the crisp fried chicken
those spare ribs and pork chops
roast turkey   wild duck larded with bacon
and bursting with onion stuffing
Hurry! Hurry! Bring on slices of
rare roast beef oozing juices as
the Chef cuts ruby-deep and thick
I have no rivals here   no need to share
No-one to admonish "watch your weight"
there is no need to defer to others
The pangs of hunger gnaw at my entrails
and I am alone at the groaning board
while the aroma of spices fills the air
tantalizes the palate   the insatiable appetite
Now with ringed fingers I shall approach
the Brownies   their fudge-frosting inches thick
truffles and tarts   mincepies   pecan pies
applepie very much a la mode   cakes

to make a weaker stomach cringe before
their mountains of rich icing   each cake
a masterpiece of haute cuisine!
Eat more! Eat more! my eager audience cries
We love your cushioned hips   your melon breasts
Queen of Corpulence!   Empress of Gastronomie!
<u>You are beautiful!</u>
Here Diet is a dirty word
a salacious word
gone forever from my vocabulary
along with scales and measurements and calories!
Dream on   Live on forever Paradise of Pastries
Oasis of Olefactory joy, my Life, my Love!
I revel in your promises

News Item

The Art Gallery must move
the building was put up
in the late Sixties
State of the Art at that time
it would be prohibitive
to update the aging edifice
Hold on a minute!
nineteen-sixty was
a very short time ago
only yesterday it seems
this newscast offends me
suggesting such decrepitude
that I am forced to wonder
if I
will be standing tomorrow!

(IV)

The Myth Of Love

The Myth Of Love: I
Prince Charming

When Prince Charming
drives up to the door
we're ready for him
we know what to expect
    all that gallantry
those promises of
never-ending devotion
we endow our Prince with
everything he needs
to make us happy and of course
his adoration will endure
forever!
Raised on Fairy Tales
on Harlequin Romance   and Soaps
how could we ever doubt it?
Awakening will come later
not with that first fabulous kiss
but slowly over time
with slips and slides

mistakes and misery
with doubts and accusations
The Prince has warts
the Prince gets tired
he's even cross at times
well   so are we!
the last Prince
made me laugh   we shared
our frailties

88

The Myth Of Love: II
Natural History

With scorpions and spiders
it is the female
that after consummation
ferociously eats the male
is this the reason that
men love women but never
like or trust them?
did this mix
of love and antipathy
evolve mechanically
from the gases and dust
of the solar system
a soup of chemicals with
the essentials for life
rising from primordial ooze
in a slow progression
of propagation
First attraction and compulsion
then revulsion and death

so relationships are doomed
before they are begun   and
have we no say in the matter?
Though our brains have
grown larger over time
is modern woman still
powerless over destiny   and
what about the unfortunate male
shouldn't he
being victimized by destiny
have some of our pity?

90

The Myth Of Love: III
Lover, Goodbye

I am in mourning today
I have buried someone
very dear to me
tomorrow when you see him
you will be surprised
at how well he looks and
think I have told a lie
Oh! he is handsome and
when he smiles at you
his teeth are beautiful
his rich voice would charm
birds from the trees
I am reluctant to lose
such a fine lover but
it is a necessity
last night he committed
The unforgivable sin
my god! how he bored me!

The Myth Of Love: IV
Promises

you said
till death and after
then turned
to rock all heaven
with crazy laughter

92

The Myth Of Love: V
Dialogue

Open your eyes
Sleeping Beauty
open them wide
why are you dreaming so deeply
when love is waiting outside?

 Mother dear Mother
I do not sleep
the nightmares are real
the heartache deep
the past is dead
and it can't return
if an old love's fire
has ceased to burn
Try to accept
that now for me
it's only the future
I would see
Waken dear Mother
open your eyes
ahead, far ahead
my dreamland lies

(I)
SURVIVAL

(II)
VIGNETTES

(III)
A LITTLE ELOCUTION

(IV)
THE MYTHS OF LOVE